Character

D1535685

CATAROTTI
Suave, debo
He likes to ho
A huge appe
And a great set of lungs!

DANDIE KATT
With a voice that's so sweet,
You'll hear it and sigh;
This pre-"Madonna"
Is one cutie pie!

THE WEE LITTLE KITTENS
Litter mates and little messes,
Day and night—always restless.
Jumping, rolling, filled with glee,
So full of life—"C'est la vie!"

CALICO
A fabulous feline,
Who's graceful, yet bold,
Companion and champion,
Her voice is pure gold.

BERNIE BOY
Head in the clouds,
Feet off the ground,
He gets into trouble
When no one's around.

THE LANE CHAPEL CATS
Four cool cats,
How they harmonize.
That they sing for their supper
Is not a surprise!

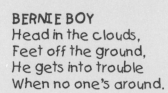

Cat Hymns

Lyrics by
Stephen & Patti Thompson

Arranged by Cindy Murphy
Illustrated by Bruce Bigelow

QUAIL RIDGE PRESS

Dedication

To Puff Puff, whose spirit has watched over this endeavor from the very beginning, and to the feline companions that allow us to share their home: Krispy Kritter, Sister Verry Merry Phyllis, A.J., Mama Kitty, Spike, O.J., and Tazz.

Acknowledgment

We are indebted to the many wonderful humans who lent their talented paws to make this project possible: Cindy Murphy, our publicist, agent, and friend, who served patiently as the musical director for Cat Hymns, the compact disc; Bruce Bigelow, from Sundown Studio, for his colorful illustrations that even under cat-o-strofic deadlines brought purr-sonality and life to all the Cats of Character; Wayne Murphy for his sense of humor, his professional manner, and his many talents in mixing the "caterwauling" from numerous weeks of digital recording in his studio at Performance Services; Gwen and Barney McKee and the understanding staff at Quail Ridge Press for their encouragement and faith in this project; Michael Graham, principal musician and major musical genius; all those who sang (see footnotes of each song); and last, but not least, our families and co-workers who understood our devotion to helping animals, and covered for all the times we were away working on Cat Hymns.

Library of Congress Cataloging-in-Publication Data

Thompson, Stephen Curtis, 1952-
    Cat hymns / by Stephen & Patti Thompson.
        p.   cm.
    ISBN 0-937552-88-7
    1. Cats-Poetry. 2. Humorous poetry, American. 3. Parodies.
  I. Thompson, Patti, 1955-   .   II. Title.
  PS3570.H64367C3 1997
  811'.54--dc21   97-6773
                                              CIP

Chow, Purina, Cat Chow, Kitten Chow, and the 3-row checkerboard design are registered trademarks of Ralston Purina Company. Cheerios is a registered trademark of General Mills Inc. and is used with their permission.

Copyright © 1997
by Stephen Thompson
CD copyright by Performance Services
ISBN 0-937552-88-7
All rights reserved
Printed in South Korea

Contents

Foreword

I love hymns ... and I love cats. So it comes as no surprise to my husband, Stephen, that I sing cat hymns to my cats. I'll hear a lovely old hymn at church and sort of rephrase it to suit the antics my cats are up to at the time. Actually, that's just how *Cat Hymns* came about. We came home one Sunday afternoon and found our "scare-dy cat," A.J., stuck in a tree. To soothe him, I began to sing the closing hymn from that morning's service. "Just As I Am, Alone in this tree, The bird got away, O woe is me ...." Stephen got all goose bumpy and said, "Patti, this is golden." And so it began. Stephen, who has been writing songs for about four years now, grabbed a pen and jotted down what I sang. "Another verse!" he would beg. For the next couple of weeks I would see him with pen in hand ready to tackle any snippet of cat songs I could produce and he could finish. We both cried when I showed him the words to "A Shining Place," a song I comforted myself with on the day my beloved Puff-Puff was released from this world. I still cannot hear anyone sing it without tears falling.

We began singing our *Cat Hymns* to friends and family, and the response was overwhelming. Through a series of magical circumstances and providence (Puff told God about us!), we met just the right people in the music, graphics, recording and publishing businesses, and this whole project came together quickly with more excitement and fun, love and surprises than we could imagine! (Little did we know that *we* would be singing and recording some of the hymns ourselves as Gwenipurr and Mr. Lucky.) We are privileged to share *Cat Hymns*, with the hope that our Sunday afternoon enjoyment will entertain you as well.

We will donate 10% of our royalties from the sale of *Cat Hymns* to the Humane Society. In addition, our publisher will donate a portion of their proceeds to the A.S.P.C.A. Over the years, I have worked closely with the Tupelo-Lee Humane Society, and I love to watch others discover what I've known all along ... shelter adoptees and strays do make the best companions and loyal life-long friends. I pray that *Cat Hymns* will charm you into visiting your local animal shelter. Who knows? You could find a purr-fectly wonderful friend waiting for you in the *"Row of Cages."*

We hope *Cat Hymns* will help you celebrate those creatures that many believe to be one of God's most challenging and adorable creations—certainly the cats think this is true.

Meow!
Patti & Stephen Thompson

4

I Will Sing of My Purina
(I Will Sing the Wondrous Story)

I will sing of my Purina®,
    How it beats most anything.
There ain't nothing else above it,
    Purina is the one for me!

    Yes, I'll sing - - - - - - of my Purina,
      (Yes, I'll sing)   (of my Purina,)
    Buy it now - - - - - - buy it for me.
      (Buy it now)   (buy it for me.)
    Serve it with - - - - - -some milk and honey,
      (Serve it with)   (some milk and honey,)
    Serve it dry - - - - - - Bon appetit!
      (Serve it dry)   (Bon appetit!)

I was lost, but Missus found me,
    Took me when I was a stray.
Threw her loving arms around me,
    Now it's Purina all the day!

She will feed me beef and liver,
    Bowls of chowder at my feet,
Then it's time for my Purina,
    Still my favorite thing to eat!

Oh They Tell Me of a Home
(Oh They Tell Me of a Home)

Oh they tell me of a home
    Where a kind lady lives,
    And she feeds all her cats twice a day.
Oh they tell me of a home
    In the countryside,
    Oh they tell me that she takes in strays.

    Oh a home that takes in strays,
    Oh a home for us castaways;
    Oh they tell me of a home in the countryside,
    Oh they tell me that she takes in strays.

Oh they tell me of a home
    Where my friends have gone,
    And it really isn't very far away;
Oh they tell me of a home
    Where there is no broom,
    Oh they tell me that she takes in strays.

Oh they tell me that she smiles
    On her kittens there,
    And she drives all the bad dogs away;
And they tell me that no tears
    Ever come again,
    Oh they tell me that she takes in strays.

Song #2. Performed by the Catler Brothers Quartet (The Gusmus Grass).

CATNIP
XXX

Lord, I'm Coming Home
(Lord, I'm Coming Home)

I've wandered far from my own yard,
    Now I'm coming home;
The paths of sin have made me tired,
    Lord, I'm coming home.

    Coming home, coming home,
    Never more to roam,
    Open wide thine arms of love,
    Lord, I'm coming home.

You act like I've been gone for years,
    Now I'm coming home;
I now repent, so dry your tears,
    Lord, I'm coming home.

I'm tired of sin, I've strayed, I'm bored,
    Now I'm coming home;
Forgive! Forget! My feet are sore!
    Lord, I'm coming home.

Song #3. Performed by Bernie Boy (Mike McIntire) and The Red Hill Mississippi Jesus New Testament Holiness Church Mass Choir.

Kittens Make the Best Companions
(Jesus Loves the Little Children)

Kittens make the best companions,
Loyal, faithful, loving friends.
    Red and yellow, black and white,
    They are creatures of the night;
Kittens make the best companions in the world!

Kittens love to live with humans,
Sharing food they keep in store:
    Milk and eggs and steak that's lean.
    Licking plates until they're clean,
Kittens make the best companions in the world!

Kittens entertain the family,
Batting balls across the den,
    Racing up and down the hall,
    Clawing paper off the wall;
Kittens make the best companions in the world!

Kittens are precious when they're sleeping;
But mischief is their middle name.
    Spreading garbage on the floor,
    Throwing up right by the door;
Kittens make the best companions in the world!

Song #4. Performed by The Wee Little Kittens (Julie Howell, Kasie Keith, Blake Kuykendall, Anna Kuykendall, Weston Murphy, Diandrea Thompson and Cayla Thompson).

There's Chow in My Bowl
(There's Power in the Blood)

Open the door, come on, let me in,
    There's Chow® in my bowl! Chow in my bowl!
Let me inside or I'll shout it again.
    There's wonderful Chow in my bowl.

    There is *Chow*, (There is Chow) *Chow*,
    Lots of Kitten Chow®
    In my bowl (In my bowl)
    On the floor (On the floor).
    There is *Chow*, (There is Chow) *Chow*,
    Lots of Kitten Chow
    In my precious bowl on the floor.

Serve me a bowl of milk on the side.
    There's Chow in my bowl! Chow in my bowl!
I'll caterwaul until I'm satisfied,
    There's wonderful Chow in my bowl.

Song #5. Performed by Catarotti (Mark Maharrey) and The Wee Little Kittens (Julie Howell, Kasie Keith, Blake Kuykendall, Anna Kuykendall, Weston Murphy, Diandrea Thompson and Cayla Thompson).

11

Oh How I Love Nap Time
(There is a Name I Love to Hear)

There is a basket I love so dear,
    I love to sleep in its berth;
It's soft and fluffy on mine ear,
    The best - est - est place on earth.

    Meow, how I love naptime,
    Meow, how I love naptime,
    Meow, how I love naptime,
    In the basket she bought for me.

It tells me of my mistress' love,
    She'd buy me anything.
It tells me I am so well thought of;
    She treats me just like a queen.

She bought my basket at the Wal-Mart,
    It's gingham and ca li co;
It's every patch is a work of art,
    Done by Michel angelo.

Song #6. Performed by Butterfly (Cindy Murphy).

I'm the Boss of the House
(Are You Washed in the Blood?)

I have shown the Missus that I have the power,
   I'm the boss of the house. Yes, I am!
I don't go 'round fussin', I just raise my brow,
   I'm the boss of the house. Yes, I am!

   I'm the boss - - - - - - - - - of the house,
     (He's the boss),   (of the house),
  Of this whole dog-gone house. Yes, I am!
                 (He's the man!)
  Oh, you may come serve me,
  It's my right, you know,
  I'm the boss of the house. Yes, I am!

I sleep till noon cometh, I stay up all night,
   I'm the boss of the house. Yes, I am!
All the meeces fear me, they stay out of sight,
   I'm the boss of the house. Yes, I am!

I don't fetch newspapers, I'm not Rin Tin Tin,
   I'm the boss of the house. Yes, I am!
I don't do the dishes. I'm the one, Meow!
   I'm the boss of the house. Yes, I am!

Song #7. Performed by Mr. Lucky (Stephen Thompson) with backup provided by Butterfly (Cindy Murphy) and Gwenipurr (Patti Thompson).

Row of Cages (Rock of Ages)

Row of cages, pardon me,
    I am lost, won't you help me?
I've got water, I've got food;
    But there's nothing I can do.
I will try, try to endure;
    Can't take more, of that I'm sure.

Could someone please let me go?
    Could somebody take me home?
Please come in, I'm all alone;
    Don't delay, I'm holdin' on.
Take my paw — to you I'll cling.
    I am lost, *please do something.*

While I draw this fleeting breath,
    Shall my eyes soon close in death?
I could die, die an unknown.
    Thou could save, and thou alone.
Row of cages, pardon me,
    I am lost, *oh please help me.*

    Song #8. Performed by the Reverend A. Jax (Tim Murfin).

Shots and Degradation
(He Keeps Me Singing)

There's within the house a mystery,
    Voices whisper really low.
I bet I'm going to the vet today,
    For some misery and woe.

    Shots and deg-ra-da-tion
    Are my lot, I know.
    I won't go out bravely,
    I'll be yowling as I go.

I smell the little can of tuna fish;
    Do you think I'm really dumb?
I saw the leash you hid behind your back,
    And there's no way I'm going to come.

Get that rubber mouse away from me,
    Stop your games and let me be.
There's no way I'll get inside that cage,
    Oops! How did you ever catch me???

Song #9. Performed by Gwenipurr (Patti Thompson).

What a Friend I Have in Catnip
(What a Friend We Have in Jesus)

What a friend I have in catnip,
    All my senses it strips bare.
What a privilege to carry
    All I can into my lair.
A,B,C's it makes me forget,
    There ain't nothin' can compare.
It beats meeces and canaries,
    Makes me dance like Fred Astaire.

Shall I give into temptation?
    It's no trouble, *au contraire*.
Let me go while I've got courage,
    I can find it — I know where.
Down the alley, by the pool hall,
    I could go get me some there.
Missus knows about my weakness,
    Breaks her heart, but I don't care.

I am weak, see how I'm fading,
    Come, show me that you still care.
Share some with me, don't be stingy,
    Oh, don't leave me in despair.
Give some to me, it won't hurt you,
    Be my friend, to you I swear,
There's no harm, let's make me feel good,
    Or I'll hock your silverware.

Song #10. Performed by Bernie Boy (Mike McIntire).

Shall We Gather at the Doghouse?
(Shall We Gather at the River?)

Shall we gather at the doghouse,
    Teasing slightly out of reach?
He'll start barking at us fiercely;
    We'll smile politely with our teeth.

    Yes, we'll gather at the doghouse.
    We'll strut our stuff, watch him cuss, doghouse.
    Raise a little cain at the doghouse
    In a game we call, "Marquis de Sade."

When we get to the doghouse,
    We'll begin to prance around.
Neighbors near it won't forgive us,
    As we torment the poor hound.

Gonna play psych with the dog, now.
    We'll be doubling his grief.
Soon our happy hearts will quiver,
    As his owner starts to screech.

Song #11. Performed by Yin and Yang (Nancy Wik).

Just As I Am (Just As I Am)

Just as I am, alone in this tree,
    The bird got away, O woe is me.
I hear you calling me, come to thee,
    O Lord, I can't ... I'm stuck. I'm stuck!

Just as I am, O my but it's dark,
    They've all gone away, they've left the park.
Well, I'd leave too, if I were smart,
    O Lord, I can't ... I'm stuck. I'm stuck!

Just as I am, tho' tossed about.
    Is anyone there to hear my shout?
I've thought 'bout taking the easy way out,
    O Lord, I can't ... I'm stuck. I'm stuck!

Song #12. Performed by Bernie Boy (Mike McIntire).

Come Home
(Softly and Tenderly)

Loudly, impatiently Missus is calling,
    Calling for you and for me;
See on the front porch she's waiting and watching,
    Watching for you and for me.

    Come home, Come home,
    I'm growing weary, come ho - o - ome.
    Loudly, impatiently Missus is calling,
    Calling O, Kitty, come home.

Why be contrary? The Missus is pleading,
    Pleading for you and for me.
Why should we linger and heed not her mercies?
    Mercies for you and for me.

Time is now fleeting, the moments are passing,
    Passing for you and for me;
Shadows are gathering, soon she'll be coming,
    Coming for you and for me.

Oh! For the wonderful food she has promised,
    Promised for you and for me;
Tho' we have hid, she has mercy and pardon,
    Pardon for you and for me.

Song #13. Performed by Mr. Lucky and Gwenipurr (Stephen and Patti Thompson), with Cindy Murphy as The Missus.

We're Climbing the Bedspread
(We're Marching to Zion)

Come cats that have grown bored,
　　Come quick! Our mistress is gone.
Stretch out a paw, eject a claw,
　　Stretch out a paw, eject a claw,
Reach out, dig in, hold on, reach out, dig in, hold on!

　　We're climbing the bedspread,
　　The beautiful, beautiful bedspread,
　　We're climbing up on the bedspread,
　　Come quick! Side by side we will fight!

Leap high and pounce around;
　　Be bold in front of our foes.
Attack and shred those fluffy things,
　　Attack and shred those fluffy things,
And watch the feathers fly, and watch the feathers fly!

What is that sound I hear?
　　Uh-oh! Her key's in the door.
She's home, oh no! We've got to go!
　　She's home, oh no! We've got to go!
Banzai, my samurai. Banzai, my samurai!

　　We've torn up the bedspread,
　　The beautiful, silk handmade bedspread.
　　We've torn, torn up the bedspread,
　　Now quick! Tell me where can we hide?

Song #14. Performed by Calico and Catarotti (Lisa Hargett and Mark Maharrey).

Cross My Paws (At the Cross)

Alas, and did my mistress grieve,
    And did my lady cry.
She got down upon both her knees,
    And begged me not to lie.

Cross my paws, cross my paws,
    I cannot tell a lie,
Have you seen all of the feathers
    on the floor?
Well, the bird got free,
    Till he passed in front of me!
I cannot tell a lie, cross my paws.

Cross my paws, cross my paws,
    I cannot tell a lie,
Did I eat your fish while you were
    at the door?
Well, as you can see,
    It's too big for me!
I cannot tell a lie, cross my paws.

Cross my paws, cross my paws,
    I cannot tell a lie,
Have you seen the vase in pieces
    on the floor?
Don't know how it cracked;
    See me rolling on my back.
I cannot tell a lie, cross my paws.

Song #15. Performed by Gwenipurr (Patti Thompson).

Meow! Why Not Tonight?
(O Why Not Tonight?)

Don't go in there. You'll be sorry.
    Don't go in there. He will hurt you.
Don't go in there. You'll be sorry.
    Don't go in there. Stay a man.

Do not let your vital parts,
    Be sterilized against the knife;
Poor Kitty, run if you are smart,
    Escape O tonight!

    Meow! Why --------- not tonight?
    Meow! Why --------- not to-night?
    Wilt thou --------- be saved?
    Escape --------- O tonight?

Tomorrow's sons may never rise,
    Express thy constituted right;
This is the time to fertilize,
    Escape O tonight!

Our wretched master is the one
    Who would from you take your birthright.
Don't let the dirty deed be done,
    Escape O tonight!

Song #16. Performed by the Reverend A. Jax (Tim Murfin).

Feline on a Stroll
(Sunshine in My Soul)

I'm a feline on a stroll today,
    O I'm such a glorious sight!
I love how girls swing and sway,
    Hoping I'll pick them tonight.

    I'm a fe --------- line,
    And I fe --------- el fine,
    I'm here! So let the good times roll;
    When I strut by, you'll want to come and play,
    I'm a feline on a stroll!

I'm a feline on a stroll today,
    O let's go frolicking.
Open your ears, listen and you'll hear,
    The girls "Ooh and aah-ing!"

I'm a feline on a stroll today,
    Lovey-dove and cuddle-up.
'Tis fate that brings you to me now,
    So come, let's fall in love!

Song #17. Performed by Mister Lucky (Stephen Thompson).

Tussle and Play (Trust and Obey)

When we're napping and bored,
    Should we frighten a bird?
Should we roar till they all fly away?
    It would give us a thrill;
Oh, it's hard to keep still,
    Free - for - all! Who will tussle and play?

    Tussle and play,
    For there's no other way
    To beat napping to pieces,
    But to tussle and play.

Not a burden or care
    While we lie here and stare,
But our boredom doth quickly go 'way.
    When we tussle and toss,
No more frowns, can't be cross,
    'Cause 'tis best if we tussle and play.

In conniption fits sweet,
    We will nip at your feet,
Or we'll claw at your side as we play.
    Oh who knows where we'll go?
Oh who knows what we'll do?
    Never fear, only tussle and play.

Song #18. Performed by Butterfly, Calico, and Gwenipurr (Cindy Murphy, Lisa Hargett, and Patti Thompson).

I Will Chase
Them Vermin
(I Am Resolved)

I am resolved no longer to hunger,
    Armed with my claws I'll smite;
Things that are smaller, Things that are older,
    I've got 'em in my sights!

    I will chase them vermin,
    Chase them so bad, yes sir-eee!
    Vermin, gratify me,
    They'll not escape from me.

I am resolved their flesh I will savor,
    Relieving them of their life;
I want to chew some, I want to crush one,
    I'll chase 'em day and night!

Fe fi fo fum, I smell a live one!
    Nothing can save its skin;
Squirrels may oppose me, crows will regret me,
    Better call their next-of-kin!

Song #19. Performed by Mr. Lucky (Stephen Thompson).

A Shining Place
(Amazing Grace)

A shining place for me to go,
    When my nine lives are gone.
They'll welcome me with open paws,
    And say, "O cat, well done!"

Cats have been here ten thousand years,
    Long before man was born,
And we'll be here until that cat,
    Gabriel blows on his horn.

The hands that held me night and day,
    I shall so sorely miss.
I still can see her standing there,
    And feel her warm last kiss.

When every cat shall be called home,
    On that bright glorious day,
We'll all join in and purr along,
    And climb heaven's gold stairway.

A shining place for me to go,
    When my nine lives are gone.
They'll welcome me with open paws,
    And say, "O cat, well done!"

Song #20. Performed by Dandie Katt (Diandrea Thompson) Verse 1; Calico and Butterfly (Lisa Hargett and Cindy Murphy) Verse 2; Butterfly, Calico, and Catarotti (Mark Maharrey) Verse 3; Calico, Butterfly, Catarotti, and Dandie Katt, Verse 4; Calico, Verse 5.

Get Up, Get Up and Feed Us
(Stand Up, Stand Up for Jesus)

Get up, get up and feed us,
　　You cannot sleep all day.
Rise high our lowly servant,
　　Rise high without delay.
Come feed us, oh come feed us,
　　Our bellies you must fill.
"Get up and go!" is our wish.
　　By now you know the drill!

Get up, get up and feed us,
　　The 'larm clock you'll obey.
Forth from your nightly slumber,
　　You must arise today.
Let "purrs" arise from our dish;
　　If not we'll bite your toes.
Come now, attend and feed us,
　　Then eat your Cheerios®!

Get up, get up and feed us,
　　It does no good to moan.
Move quickly or we'll flail you,
　　Until your bed sheet's gone.
Put on your bathrobe before,
　　The neighbors start to stare.
You're needed in the kitchen,
　　So get your butt in there!

　　Song #21. Performed by many of the Cats of Character.

Catology

(Doxology)

Praise milk from whom all blessings flow;

Praise milk, it makes my motor go;

Praise milk, I love it in my bowl;

As cream, or cheese, or à - la - mode.

Ahhhhh - milk!

TAIL NOTES

We will be happy to help you use *Cat Hymns* as a fundraiser for animal shelters or any other group that aids animals. *Cat Hymns* can be performed as a large or a small-scale production. The play, sheet music, accompaniment tracks and an instructional video are available. The authors of *Cat Hymns* may even be able to appear at these productions for book signings whenever their schedules permit. Please contact Stephen Thompson for details and availability.

mail: CAT HYMNS, P.O. Box 361, Tupelo, MS 38802
fax: 1-888-248-8379
email: cathymns@iname.com

Call Quail Ridge Press for more information about *Cat Hymns* gift items. Quail Ridge Press offers a complete line of quality books. Call or write for a free catalog of all Quail Ridge Press publications. Group and volume discounts as well as fundraiser programs are also available upon request.

mail: QUAIL RIDGE PRESS
P.O. Box 123, Brandon, MS 39043
phone: 1-800-343-1583   FAX: 1-601-825-3091
email: Info@QuailRidge.com

Cats of

MISTER LUCKY
Sometimes a sinner,
Sometimes a saint,
He's good when he's holy,
But he's great when he ain't!

BUTTERFLY
She's pampered, she's loved,
She's fed with a spoon.
She's purr-fectly content
To sleep until noon.

REVEREND A. JAX
To poor little kitties
Who've gone a-stray,
He preaches salvation ...
He shows the way.

YIN and YANG
So bad when they're naughty,
So-o-o polite when they're nice.
Try not to cross them,
They'll make you pay twice!

GWENIPURR
Always a step
Ahead of the game,
She's witty, she's coy—
This cat's quite a dame!

SISTER VERRY MERRY PHYLLIS
A black and white cat
Who's always quite nice;
To save the homeless
Is her mission in life.

CATLER BROTHERS' QUARTET
A four-cat quartet
That sings 'round the world
Four strays—all "toms,"
('Cept one is a girl!)